Carrying On Easily

Steps To Coping With Stress
The Fun, Achievable And
Timely Way

By
Fhilcar Faunillan

Fhilcar Faunillan

Carrying on Easily

The information provided herein is stated to be truthful and consistent, in that any liability, in terms of inattention or otherwise, by any usage or abuse of any policies, processes, or directions contained within is the solitary and utter responsibility of the recipient reader. Under no circumstances will any legal responsibility or blame be held against the publisher for any reparation, damages, or monetary loss due to the information herein, either directly or indirectly.

Respective authors own all copyrights not held by the publisher.

The information herein is offered for informational purposes solely, and is universal as so. The presentation of the information is without contract or any type of guarantee assurance.

The trademarks that are used are without any consent, and the publication of the trademark is without permission or backing by the trademark owner. All trademarks and brands within this book are for clarifying purposes only and are the owned by the owners themselves, not affiliated with this document.

Table of Contents

INTRODUCTION

I want to thank you and congratulate you for downloading the book, *"Carrying On Easily:* Steps to Coping with Stress the Fun, Achievable, and Timely Way*".*

As part of the throng of people living in today's ultra-competitive and demanding environment, we do our best to meet expectations in hopes of securing a brighter future for ourselves and for our loved ones. We do overtime work to get some extra income but at the expense of precious rest time or opportunities to bond with friends and family.

Maybe you are a graduating student currently working on your thesis a.k.a. your defining moment in your entire academic existence. Like an employee tendering in some overtime hours, you fight tooth and nail, exhaust your blood, sweat, and tears to make sure your thesis is the best that it can be. Once again, you do this at the expense of what could have been time to spend with the people around you or the opportunity to try new things.

Lucky for you, though, if you are the type of person who practices time management. But a whole lot of people do not engage in this behavior. Why? Simply because it is tedious. It involves limiting yourself somehow. But is it necessary?

Some people can only function with the help of a to-do list to guide them throughout the day, while others find some kind of peace in the chaos of trying to find out what to do next as the day passes. The point here is that someone's coping mechanism may not be applicable to another.

This book you now have in your hands will not stick you with only a few coping mechanisms that are only applicable to a select few. In these pages are numerous ways of coping suited to your personality, capability, and attitude! Every single point given in this book is so easy to grasp and can easily be applied to your chosen coping plan.

You must remember, though, that whatever coping strategy you plan to use will require your full commitment in order to work for you and help you relieve your stress. So if you are all set to start your journey to a lessened-stress life, turn this page and carry on!

Thanks again for downloading this book, I hope you enjoy it!

Chapter 1- Know Your Enemy

Stress is something we have all felt at more than one point in our lives. As children, we have experienced stress in the form of anxiety when we temporarily lose track of our parent in a crowd. We feel stressed in the form of guilt when we are reprimanded for doing something wrong. We feel stressed in the form of fear when we are chased by our neighbor's dog. In all these occasions, incessant cries are the usual coping mechanism we readily use to ease the anxiety, guilt or fear.

As students in every year level of school, stress is felt whenever there are loads and loads of schoolwork to be done and you feel like you have absolutely no time to finish them all and turn them in when you should. Coping with such may be done through procrastination or staying up late into the night or foregoing sleep altogether.

Not only do we suffer stress from academics while growing up but we also experience stress from peer pressures and social circles. We feel stressed when we cannot keep up with our peers or when we feel that we belong nowhere. The things that teenagers do to cope with these kinds of stresses can be varied, strange and almost always harmful to themselves. For instance, they start smoking, start drinking and even engage in unsafe sexual behaviors.

And then we have the different coping strategies we use as adults faced with all kinds of stress. An ugly encounter at work can be coped with by writing a long rant on social media (making sure to hide this from the person at the opposite side of the encounter, of course). A recent break-up becomes a reason to lounge all day in front of the television, munching on every junk food known to man with a side of pints and pints of ice cream.

Truly, stress is a daily occurrence and we often experience them even when we fail to acknowledge the event as stressful. This is why as we age, we develop different coping mechanisms to deal with these environmental stressors. These coping mechanisms may be beneficial, temporarily relieving, all-out avoidant, or simply harmful to ourselves. However, these poor and harmful coping mechanisms, instead of getting rid of the stress you are in, may just add to the stress and put you in a more intensified rut.

You may have opened this book with the expectation of immediately finding out how you can cope with the different stressors in your life; but before learning about coping mechanisms, you have to know your enemy first. There are some things you have to do before the actual coping.

Right now, as you read this book in your hands, can you identify every single thing that causes stress in your life? You may find that you are stressed by the fact that the coffee shop is too hot for your liking or the coffee you ordered wasn't that well-prepared. And then you realized that your boyfriend hasn't texted in full five hours and you thought that it was maybe your fault when you shouted at him in the morning. And then there is that girl with an annoying laugh in the corner...you may find that it is actually difficult to list them all down because stressors tend to be consciously overlooked when, in fact, they have been haunting you like a looming ghost that is out to make your life like hell.

For instance, you may have recognized that work or school deadlines are quite the source of immense stress to you. You may have failed to realize, though, that the actual cause of the stress you have been feeling is your procrastination which leads to working just right before a

deadline. Does this sound like something you have been feeling lately or for years?

To be able to correctly identify whatever it is that gets you all stressed out, you need to take a closer look at your attitude and your habits. Are you the type of person who believes that a certain stressor is uncontrollable believing that you are fat because you just have fat genes? Or are you just an innately anxious person who has but negative thoughts of the future? Does the stress you feel come from outside of you or from the innermost parts of your being?

Something that may help you out in your quest to finding out what causes you stress is to keep a journal or diary. You do not have to sound all literary when you write on your journal; just write your heart and mind out. Writing is a very helpful exercise because it allows you to think about the problem differently. When the ball point hits the paper, you write out of frustration or anger at first. Eventually though, you begin writing about the reasons of your frustration or anger making you become aware of your emotions. You may even find yourself more relaxed after doing some journaling because, in some way, you have let out your frustrations.

After getting to know what makes you all stressed out, you need to take a look at how you currently cope with stress. It would be ideal to write these down in your journal as well for proper monitoring or just plain reminiscing. How had you reacted when the pizza delivery guy was late for ten minutes when you were starving? How had you reacted to negative comments about you from others? How had you reacted to the news of the death of a close relative? You may be surprised at how you have actually been dealing with stress these past few years.

Let's face it, we sometimes cope with stress through unhealthy means like binge watching shows for days on one end or maybe you resort to drinking like there's no tomorrow. While both watching TV and drinking are not inherently bad things for you and are even beneficial when done at a leisurely pace, forgoing daily activities which are of greater importance in favor of doing only these activities alone is something you should not consider as a coping mechanism in the long run.

Always remember that the most important person in this journey of properly coping with stress is YOU. In order for this book to effectively help you out, you need to accept that some of your current stress management strategies or lack thereof are not good for you. You need to start thinking about what is best for you in all aspects. Do remember that you are not being selfish, since some people tend to hesitate doing something good for themselves due to others judging them of being self-centered instead of in need of some self-love and support. Lastly, you need to be open to change, be it big or small. Are you up for that? If your answer is yes, then continue on to the next chapters and begin treading the path to a life of better coping.

Chapter 2 - Avoid the Void

One common mechanism that people use to deal with a stressful life is by actually avoiding that which makes them feel stressed. Today when there are many jobs that only require a minimal set of skills, one can now quit a job when the working environment does not suit him or her because he or she can now find another job anyway. Another example of this coping mechanism is divorce. When you do not like your spouse anymore and the sight of him or her stresses you, you can avoid your spouse and permanently remove him or her from your life through divorce.

Avoidance as a coping mechanism is not only used in big-time life changes but is also applicable to small but important tasks as well. A very common example of this would be avoiding doing the dishes, laundry, or cleaning of the house especially when you are living alone. This kind of coping mechanism sounds simple and, in some ways, people take the easy route of just full-on leaving their stressor behind. While doing this may be beneficial when done for only a limited amount of time such as avoiding continuing a task in order to get back to work feeling more energized, some may opt to avoid and forget for more time than necessary, resulting to more stress due to a growing backlog of tasks yet to be finished.

Most stressors may actually come out of the very things we deal with every day like work, family and friends, the daily commute, or even yourself. It is true that you cannot just eliminate these stress-inducing things from your life, but you may minimize the way you get all stressed out by them by knowing what makes you tick and taking some control of a stressful situation.

Here are some key points to remember as you cope with stress using avoidance:

1.) Take control

Some aspects of a stressor may be easily avoided. For instance, if being caught in traffic leaves you all hot and bothered, take a less-busy route or travel earlier than most people. If a co-worker has been offending you with ruthless remarks, request a transfer to another department or branch.

The changes that need to be done to avoid stressors can be as simple as dimming the lights when bright bulbs become irritating or as complicated as switching to a more comfortable toilet. When you start taking control of your life, you will realize that all the stresses you have been experiencing in the past are partly of your making. Just remember your end-goal of a life with less stress and you may start seeing that these changes are not so difficult to undertake.

2.) No means no

In a world that appreciates being helped out, you may sometimes find yourself unable to refuse someone in need of your help. Or maybe you are piled up with more work than you can handle because you do not want to let someone down. "No" is your magic word in these trying times.

We all have a superhero complex of some sort in our psyche, that with pop culture perpetuating the good things that come out of being the hero (i.e. popularity, fame, etc.). But what is the use of being the hero when you are too exhausted to even enjoy the benefits? Or what is the point of being a hero when you can't even help yourself?

Know your limits and respect them. Limits do not make you any less of a person since everybody has them. Learn to gently let people down by making them understand that you are currently unable to help them but wish them the best all the same. With practice, saying "no" will come more naturally to you.

3.) Get rid of stress-inducing people

Part of knowing your limits is also coming to terms with the fact that some of the people in your life are stressors themselves. You may have tried all that you could to turn your relationship around in an effort to see the other person as less of a stressor but life is not always so giving. Some people are just simply not good for you.

If you are in a toxic relationship with someone and being with him/her is more stressful than helpful, maybe it is time that you cut that relationship for you to totally avoid that person. However, if that certain person who is stressing you out is going to be in your life for years to come, it is time that you strategize how to avoid them in an inoffensive manner.

4.) Avoid sensitive topics

Certain points of conversation can bring out the stress response in you. You may be the type to express rage towards a certain political party or maybe you are the type who would cry at the mention of a loved one who has passed. Whatever it is, do not hesitate to tell someone you are talking with to move onto another topic whenever a sensitive topic is brought up.

5.) Do only what can and should be done

Planning out your daily activities with a realistic and driven mind is important to leave out any unnecessary stress that sudden engagements can bring. Unfortunately, not all of us are filled with motivation to even get up in the morning!

A simple to-do list will suffice. The good thing about to-do lists is that it keeps your mind on your goals and the feeling of scratching items on your list is such a good feeling that there is little chance for us to avoid our tasks. Use a piece of paper and have it taped to something you constantly look at during the day like your phone or maybe a portion of your car's dashboard. For techies who are reading this book, there are a lot of to-do list apps available in the market today.

Try these:

1.) Plan your day

Most stressors that you face on a daily basis can actually be avoided by doing some meticulous planning before your day starts. For instance, you want to avoid an offensive coworker at lunch break who always seems to want to sit with you at the pantry. Try working an earlier or later lunch time for yourself into your daily plan, without regard for your workplace's mandated lunch time, of course.

Using this coping strategy will not only help you avoid stressors (e.g. offensive coworker), you will also be able to exert some control on how your day goes. This feeling of control is something considered precious to any person under immense stress and feels like he or she cannot do anything about his or her situation.

2.) Create a "letting down" script

The "letting down" described here is and should not be equated to failing someone; rather, think of this "letting down" as a way of not failing yourself.

For example, you have been having the hardest time turning down a friend's invitations to brunch where you end up paying for so much more than your budget can accommodate. This friend is someone you hold so close to your heart but you need to think of the needs you are neglecting as you spend insane amounts of money on some fancy bagel you do not even like.

Find some time to sit yourself down, a sheet of paper and a pen in front of you. Write down a script detailing what you will say in refusal of your friend's invitation without foregoing kindness and conscientiousness. Make the script short yet sincere as much as possible.

3.) Travel far, travel near

Now, hold up. A lot of us would be so game for some travel time, especially in some faraway, fantasy destination we have always dreamed of visiting. This would cost us so much money and a lot of time for planning, though.

While an extended vacation is not exactly possible for you at the moment, a weekend getaway is the next best thing. Traveling to a nearby place should not be underestimated. Why, you ask?

The key thing about going away for a little while is to try and distance yourself from any source of immediate stress, may it be at work or at school or maybe in the home. You can go on this short-term journey alone or with a friend, too.

4.) Set a "cry" hour

Let's face it: we need a good cry every once in a while. But present circumstances may be barring you from letting those tears flow. For instance, you are in the middle of a meeting when, just a while ago, your ideas were rudely rejected. What do you do to stem the flow of tears from your already swelling eyes?

You tell yourself to delay your crying time for a later hour – an hour we shall call the "cry hour". Whatever frustrating events that may happen to you throughout the day, delay your cry response and save them for your cry hour.

You are now home and sitting on your bed. Set a gentle alarm on your phone for one hour. Place your phone aside, put your hands in front of your face, and wail. Wail like you have never wailed before. Let all those tears gush freely from your eyes that have exhausted themselves trying to hold those tears in for hours on end.

Cry for everything that bothered you that day. Cry for everything that has been bothering you for a longer time since then. Cry for all the upcoming stress you will be experiencing. Cry for the fact that you are crying at this very moment, forgetting to even change out of your work clothes. Cry for everything. Cry for nothing. Cry until you aren't. And then cry some more.

Is your hour finally up? If not, go ahead and check if you still have any "cry" to give. Remember the feeling of relief or emptiness or whatever catharsis you are experiencing at this moment. Tell yourself that achieving this feeling is good and very much attainable. Being okay is something that is bound to happen.

Chapter 3 - Make a Change

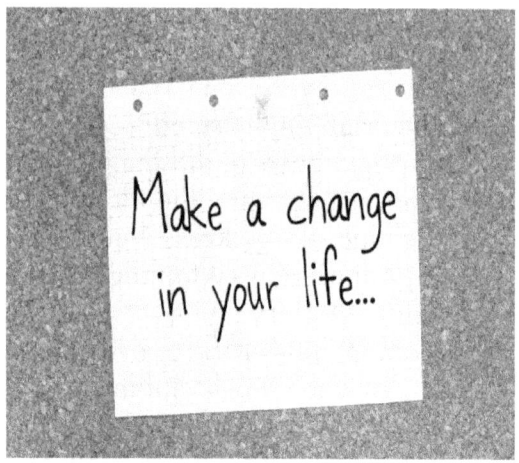

The previous chapter talked about the value of avoiding unnecessary stress. But it is a fact of life that not all stressors are avoidable. Because of this, you need to know how to change something about a stressful situation in order to avoid actually dealing with stress in the first place.

Perhaps your partner's tendency to be late when you go out on dates has been bothering you for quite some time. You may think that your partner does not care enough for you in this regard, but have you ever actually thought of turning this around? Don't you think that you can put a stop to the disappointment you feel?

This change may be undertaken in so many ways but learning the following traits is especially important since they help in welcoming more healthy coping mechanisms in the long run:

1.) Assertiveness

You may oftentimes find yourself stressed out by things that do not necessarily jive with what you believe is right. Assertiveness is most needed in this case. You need not fear how others will see you when you go against them since you know in your heart of hearts that you are right. You must know how to stand your ground amidst temptation to go with the norm.

While you may feel that what you are fighting for is correct, this does not give you the right to gloat. When asserting yourself, you need to be careful with the words you use. Practice empathy by placing yourself in the other's shoes and see whether the way you plan to assert yourself is just right or too aggressive.

Becoming assertive is often confused with becoming aggressive. Do not fall for this false belief since there is a fine line between these two concepts. Assertiveness involves calmly making your point without putting down or belittling another person and his or her ideas. Aggression, on the other hand, is characterized by trying to prove that you are right without any regard whatsoever for another person's feelings. You push and you push and, eventually, something will have to give when you practice aggression.

Using the tardy partner example mentioned above, the right way to assert would be to sit your partner down and just tell him or her directly about the problem. Do this in a calm voice while exuding an easy yet serious demeanor. If your partner starts reasoning with you, answer him or her accordingly without ever raising your voice or feeling offended. Remember that respect should be afforded to everybody at all times.

2.) Compromise

If something about a person stresses you out, you might tell him or her to change his or her ways. In the spirit of compromise, you should be all in when it comes to changing your ways as well. This is all about having mutual respect with the other.

Take the tardy partner example stated above. You have decided to tell your partner about how bad you feel every time he or she comes late for a date or meet-up. You used the first lesson in this chapter, assertiveness, to bring your dilemma to a resolution. But your partner has a concern of his or her with regards to a behavior you have been exuding as well.

Maybe your partner feels bad that you did not tell him or her immediately about how his or her tardiness bothered you. Taking compromise into action, you need to set a deal with your partner; you promising to be more open about your feelings and your partner committing to lessen and altogether eliminating his tendency to be late.

3.) Expression of feelings

Whenever you feel bothered by a stressor in your life, it may be beneficial for you to voice out your concerns and sentiments. Do remember that you should air these out in the most respectful way you can possibly muster. This will help you in getting rid of budding resentments that can bring about stress.

If you happen to be in a situation like the tardy partner predicament discussed above, expressing your feelings about your partner's behavior is the first step in resolving whatever stress you have. Just be sure to be direct when you communicate your concerns so that your partner can change his or her ways accordingly.

4.) Time Management

In order to stay focused on a task instead of being stressed out by too many tasks all at once, time management can become your best friend. Not only will you be able to avoid the stress brought about by rush, you will also find that you have some time for less stressful activities during your day.

Time management involves organizing and planning how much time you will be spending on doing a given task. Practicing time management can lead you to become more productive and efficient. You will also have a better reputation as a professional, gaining the trust of your superiors at work or in your organization.

Failure to manage your time properly can result to missed deadlines which can also mean missed opportunities. Your work can become mediocre at best, your stress levels heightened, and your professional reputation not so favorable.

Investing some of your time and effort to planning your daily, weekly, or monthly activities can be good for you in the long run when maintained. Not only will you be generally less stressed, your career will also flourish because of this new skill.

Try these:

1.) Wear your workout clothes to bed

Say you have been stressed out due to your lack of exercise and physical activity for the past few months. Maybe this is because to sheer exhaustion or just a lack of motivation to get up extra early in the morning to change into your workout attire.

To address these concerns, try sleeping in your workout clothes. That way, you do not have to try lugging your body towards your closet to get your clothes only to find out that you fell back asleep while trying to find what to wear.

By doing a minor change in the form of wearing something different to bed, you can start applying major changes to other aspects of your life knowing that you have succeeded in maintaining this one.

2.) Take up an expressive hobby

Doing work and only work alone is not a life that one should live. Rather, sometime must be allotted to leisure and doing something fun yet cathartic. This is where an expressive hobby comes in.

Try chronicling your daily life or your feelings or whatever it is you want to get out of your chest and express all of this by writing a diary or blog, video-blogging or vlogging, writing and performing slam poetry, or by painting.

Now that you have chosen your expressive hobby, incorporate this into your daily or weekly routine. Not only does this method help in releasing any tensions within you, you are also driven to follow a schedule, strengthening your time management skills. When you look over your finished work for the day or week, you will feel less stressed and more ready to take on whatever challenges life has in store for you.

3.) Clean your room

While this may sound all chore-like, you do not need to clean your entire room all in one sitting. In fact, if you are not bothered by any means by your room's current state, you do not have to continue reading this portion.

But for a number of us, our rooms are left in a mess that we cannot handle due to being left alone thanks to stress. But say you have identified your room as a stressor and have chosen to make a change about it. What is the best way of going about this without having to use up all your time for the day?

Simply choose just a section of your room to clean for a certain amount of time. You may even opt to clean your room only until a chosen song of yours finishes. The point here is that you do not need to do any drastic changes overnight. Gradual steps will get you somewhere closer to where you want to be. Just be patient with yourself and the pace you are progressing.

Chapter 4- The Need for Acceptance

Stress is felt when a person feels like they are incapable of achieving a certain goal. Well, imagine not just feeling incapable but actually being incapable of doing something you desire to do? That is a whole lot of stress you have on your already-filled plate.

We often hear the words "life is unfair" or "life is rarely kind" and these are truths that we need to take by heart, but you need to remember that this is not because life has some kind of grudge against you, life just does things regardless of how you feel about them. Life is a thrill. Embrace it.

In order to somehow erase some of the stress you are in, start accepting that some things are just out of your control. If a favorite band of yours decides to break-up and go on solo careers instead, accept it. Maybe you have a friend who is so excited to get a tattoo and you, a hypothetically anti-tattoo person, cannot do anything about it. Accept it. Accept it wholeheartedly.

Some important points you need to remember when treading the path of acceptance are:

1.) The uncontrollable is UN-CONTROLLABLE.

Once you acknowledge that something bugging you in your life is out of your control, acceptance is the surefire way to combat any future stress. There is no use in trying to worry about changing something that simply cannot be changed.

For instance, a certain friend's trait is bothering you. Rather than getting all stressed out by this, try changing how you react to that particular trait in your friend. While the central stressor may be uncontrollable, your reactions to it are totally in your hands. Use it to your advantage.

2.) There is a bright side to everything.

If you find yourself in a particularly stressful situation, chances are that you regret doing what got you there in the first place. Instead of waddle in your sea of regret, try learning from your wrong decision. Or maybe stop thinking of your decision as "wrong" and more as "less right".

The stress brought about by whatever is testing you right now can be channeled positively by thinking of your predicament as a window of opportunity to try new things, discover yourself, or just plainly have fun.

Take the disbanding of your favorite musical group as an example. Perhaps you have a favorite member among them who has wanted for so long to pursue a career in acting but was unable to due to the band's high demand. Now that they have disbanded, your favorite member's acting career may just be a reality. Isn't that something to feel happy about?

3.) Forgiveness is your best friend.

Holding grudges is an invitation for stress to invade your being. While it is healthy to feel some resentment towards someone who has done you wrong, holding on to it for too long is destructive. Accept that people make mistakes.

More importantly, forgive someone who wronged you

because you care about yourself. Withholding forgiveness and holding onto grudges can make you more depressed or anxious and unable to enjoy your life at present. The idea that self-care is a necessity will help you forgive easily, without excusing the wrongful act, of course.

When you forgive someone, you need to distance yourself from feeling like a victim of the wrongful act. You need to release your grudges' hold on you. So go on and rethink about some recent hurts you have been feeling and begin the process of forgiving the one who hurt you. Not only will this lift a burden off of the other person's shoulders, but you will become free of all the stress and lingering hurt that, in fact, you do not need to be carrying with yourself forever.

4.) Talk about how you feel

Part of making acceptance of an unchangeable thing easier is by talking about your current situation with a trusted friend or family member. This helps in further acknowledging the stress that you are in and, in turn, the person you are sharing your sentiments to will be able to remind you that your aggravation is valid.

You may also write out your feelings through a diary or a blog. You can even do a recording of just your voice or a full-blown video complete with sentimental music! But, kidding aside, it is important that you somehow release your frustrations in some way, for as long as you know that your potential audience is made up of people you trust and who understand and love you for who you are.

Try these:

1.) Swear your lungs out

The stress you are feeling can be too much at times. One great way of relieving some of this inner tension is by screaming at the top of your lungs. You can even take this up a notch by using all the swear words in your vocabulary.

You and a friend can go to an elevated area like a mountain or a rooftop. Count to three and just scream! Let all of your feelings out. Do not hold back. If you need to take a breather before continuing, do so. Just make sure that, in some way, you are able to let out your frustrations.

An alternative to swearing loudly is by crying your eyes out. Resist any urge to hold back and just let the tears flow. You may not be expressing any words but some of the heart-wrenching feelings you are experiencing will be shed by a once-in-a-while cry-fest.

2.) Go down a slide

As a practice of relinquishing control over something beyond your means, visit a playground or water park that has slides in it. Go down the slide without putting up any resistance with your hands or whatever else can slow you down. Just let gravity bring you to the bottom.

You see here that not trying to control the speed at which you are going down the slide does not just free you of any anxiety and hassle of trying to produce friction with such slippery surfaces, you are also able to let go and just enjoy the thrill of the ride down the slide. It also helps that slides remind you of such fun times as a kid.

3.) Write a letter

Let's say you just walked out of a group meeting after one of your teammates made an offensive remark that bothered you to no end. You are absolutely fuming with anger at this person, right?

Instead of letting your frustrations out by cursing like a mad man or woman in public, how about writing a letter instead? In this letter, write every single detail of your frustration towards this person. Write how you want to react, write about how frustrated you feel at the thought of not being able to do so.

Continue writing about whatever your heart is currently struggling to feel and come to terms with. After letting your feelings out, write how you will be forgiving this person. You probably did not see that one coming, though.

Why would a letter filled with so much hate turn into one of forgiveness? As mentioned earlier in the chapter, the need to forgive should not stem from some sense of duty you feel towards the person who wronged you; rather, you need to forgive for the sake of you and your well-being.

This letter to your offender will serve as an attempt at reaching some inner peace without having to do something damaging like screaming at the other person in public, risking not only his or her reputation, but yours as well.

Now sign the letter with your name and a double-meaning doodle if you wish. Fold it and throw it away. Whatever happens, do not send this to your offender. You will have more time to think about forgiving him or her after, anyway.

Chapter 5- Be the Change

Sometimes, in life, stressors are just plain unavoidable. You may have tried to change something about the stressful situation at hand but have found that you can only do so much. When something proves to be unchangeable, there's only one other thing you can do: *become the change*.

What makes a stressor so stressful is actually your appraisal of it. Thus, changing how you view the different stress-inducing things of this life is detrimental in better coping with stress as a whole. What is expected to change in this respect are your reactions and attitudes towards a stressor.

Below are some of the common yet important ways that you can begin changing how you treat the different stressors you encounter every day:

1.) See things differently

Imagine yourself stuck in a long line at a fast food joint and you have decided to stay there no matter what. Sure, the sumptuous burger and fries combo you will be ordering may be worth the wait, but the wait will last for quite a while. Instead of getting all bummed out due to the long line or the packed crowd, try seeing the waiting time as an opportunity to rethink some future plans you might have.

Maybe you can plan out how exactly you will be consuming the burger once you finally have it in your hands. Will you eat your way from front to back or nibble as you rotate your burger? Maybe you want to eat the bread first and the bun last?

Being able to change how you see commonly stressful things can really help you avoid getting all flustered. You just need to make your mind see the good in everything you face.

2.) Take a second glance

Is that thing you are stressing over really worth being bothered about? Will all this anxiety matter in the future? You need to ask yourself these questions in order to really put your situation into a broader perspective. If you answered no to both questions, then maybe you need to channel your focus on something else more important than what you are currently worrying about.

For instance, you have been worried about attending a reunion your ex is sure to attend. While your breakup may not have been bad enough to make you not want to attend the said event, you still feel the scars of your parting as if they were put there yesterday.

Here you are, worried about bumping into this ex of yours. The thing is, though, you can never predict what will actually happen. You have sacrificed so much time for sleep obsessing over seeing him or her, looking like you were a thing of a past that he or she could not care less about.

Are you really going to let this one probable incident of bumping into your ex get in the way of you enjoying the reunion with the rest of your friends? Will all this anxiety even do you any good? If you really look at it, you do not have a hold on how you and your ex will be like once you run into each other. So let go of any worry and focus instead on the positives the reunion will bring.

3.) Be realistic

Oftentimes we are bothered by our inner-perfectionists. While feeling some self-doubt is normal and even healthy at times (since it drives you to improve yourself and your work), becoming a slave to unrealistic expectations will get you nowhere.

Becoming the best is not at all the worst thing, but so is being "good enough". It helps to remember that we, as humans, are prone to imperfections. Stray away from the stress of perfectionism and start favoring reality instead.

Just imagine the immense anxiety a to-be married person is under. This person wants every single detail to be perfect. This person has forgotten, though, that he or she has little to no control over the guests coming to the wedding. This person may want his or her 3-year-old flower girl to walk a certain way but, in reality, the child will probably retain little of the instructions given to her because she is all distracted by the colorful petals in her possession. Let go of the stress by acknowledging reality and basically being chill.

4.) Pros before woes

Say you are neck-deep in a pool of stress, your time limited and your patience wearing thin. Instead of carrying on with a heavy mind and heart, try taking a break to remember all of the good sides of your current situation.

You may be in the middle of doing your thesis and have run out of any brain juices thanks to all the stress. Try looking at the upside! Your thesis is what will bring you one gigantic step closer to graduation. Or maybe your thesis is one with the potential of making a significant impact in this world.

Remember the positives; remember the reasons why you

are going through all the stress in the first place. Good vibes brought about by taking a moment to remember what matters can be the needed fuel for you to continue on and forget about your current stress.

Try these:

1.) Fill your life with positive affirmations

You have seen the framed, cross-stitched creations that express corny messages. You have seen bumper stickers with Bible verses printed on them. You may dismiss all of these fixtures in the world around you but they do make a difference in how you see yourself or the situation at hand.

Constantly seeing these positive affirmations can solidify themselves into your psyche. Try printing out a positive message on a sticker and post it on something you are always looking at, maybe your mobile phone or your bedroom mirror. If you feel like it, you can even tattoo a dose of good vibes onto your body.

Do not underestimate the power of constant exposure. Make an effort to incorporate positive affirmations into your life and see yourself turn around and better-equipped and inspired to shake the stress away.

2.) Create a mini-bucket list

A bucket list is filled with our dreams and aspirations. While having one is good and even inspiring, oftentimes the items we list down are not readily achievable due to their expensiveness or undeniable impossibility (kiss Elvis Presley, anyone?). A little bit of reality and a good dose of rationalism shall come to rescue, then!

Instead of waiting for a long time to pass to crush one item off your bucket list, why not create a mini-bucket list? You can choose to achieve the items on a monthly or yearly basis. One has to exercise extreme realism when filling up their list so that you do not set yourself up for heartbreak due to an unattainable item you could not do due to a variety of factors.

With these being said, do not let go of your actual or main bucket list. Just be sure to stay true to your rational side while achieving your bigger-than-life dreams.

Chapter 6- No "I" in Stress

When you have been stressed out for a significant amount of time, you need to turn your mind off and relax. Engaging in some "me" time can help recharge yourself for when you need to face new battles that will come your way.

You may be thinking, though, that "me" time only constitutes visits to the spa or traveling to the world's idyllic locations. While both of these are great ways of relieving some of your stress, they are often expensive. Remember that even the simplest things can be a source of joy and breathing space.

Some people become hesitant to take some time off in fear of being seen as selfish or weak. This line of thinking needs to be stopped. Self-nurturance is a necessity that each person owes oneself. Once you internalize this belief, being able to engage in some R&R will be easier and less guilt-inducing.

The following are just some of the many ways to momentarily forget life's stresses:

1.) Set aside a time for relaxation and relaxation only

For every day that passes, include some time to do nothing; even an hour will do. During this chosen hour, block out everything that worries you and focus on staying calm. If any bothering thoughts attack you during this time, let them down gently and continue on relaxing.

2.) Stay connected

While it may be true that social media can cause a whole lot of stress and anxiety, being with people who bring you good vibes and make you forget about your troubles is something worth doing at a regular pace. Your "people" serve as buffers against stress so reach out if you must. Your whole being will thank you in the long run and, in turn, you can be a source of support for your dearest ones as well.

3.) Welcome joy

Do something you love every day. Even if this is just for a few minutes, spending some "me" time can make all the difference in keeping your sanity in check. Just as peacefulness is the goal in meditation, focus on the pure joy that your chosen leisure activity can bring.

4.) Laugh a lot

It has been scientifically proven that laughter combats stress so use this to your advantage. Laughter can release feel-good neurotransmitters in the brain which can improve our mood substantially. Aside from this, laughing also relaxes the face muscles subsequently relaxing our whole body as a result. With these benefits of stress, it is no wonder that Laughter Yoga is now a thing! So you better start laughing at not-so-funny jokes just for the sake of laughing. If you find yourself in an embarrassing situation, laugh out the stress instead of praying for the ground to swallow you whole. Here's a plus: laughing your way out of embarrassing situations can make you look confident and can make the situation more funny and less embarrassing so that can actually be good for you.

Try these:

1.) Touch, touch, touch

Use the need for stress relief as an excuse to get all touchy with your significant other! Kissing, hugging, and caressing have been shown to stimulate the release of oxytocin in the brain. This results to lowered blood pressure and calmed nerves. Taking this to the next step through sex has also been found in studies to be linked to a reduced risk in getting a heart attack or a stroke when done about three times every week. Sex has also been found to encourage the release of endorphins, improving your mood and relaxing your body.

If you are not with a significant other at this time, there is no reason to forgo this coping mechanism. Touch yourself! A simple self-massage can bring you to new heights that can help in relieving stress and ease any physical tension you are experiencing.

2.) Pressure for Pleasure

Another way of using touch to alleviate stress is by getting to know your body's different Acupressure points. Pressing on these points provides the same benefits as acupuncture, the difference lies only in that fingers are used instead of needles.

The procedure to this is to breathe deeply and then put pressure onto the following acupressure points for about two to three minutes to the point of feeling a sensation of mild ache:

• The **Hoku** is the patch of skin that connects your thumb to your pointer finger. According to studies, pressing this special part of your wrist can relieve stress as it is considered to be an acupressure spot that is mostly linked to the tension in the upper body.

• The **Heavenly Pillar** is located behind your neck, below

63

your skull's base, about half an inch to either the left or right sides of your spine. Pressure on this area can help relieve stress, over-exhaustion, insomnia, eyestrain, stiff neck, swollen eyes, and sore throat.

• The **Heavenly Rejuvenation** can be found half an inch below the topmost part of each shoulder, between the base of your neck and the outer portion of your shoulder blade. Applying pressure onto this spot can help lessen nervous tension and stiff neck while increasing your body's susceptibility to the flu. The lungs are another major beneficiary of pressure being put on this area.

• The **Third Eye** is the spot between your eyebrows, marked by a bump of some sort where your forehead and nose bridge meet. Pressing on this spot calms one's nerves.

3.) Have a one-person dance party

It may sound ridiculous at first, but do not even try to deny dancing like crazy whenever you are alone with some dance music blaring throughout your room! It is just that, this time, you are finally incorporating this activity into your coping toolkit.

Prepare a playlist of all the jams you can remember (plus points for songs that you danced to as a kid). Set aside some time, even just a few minutes, to stay alone in your room. Close all your window curtains (unless you are feeling a little adventurous at the moment), plug in your speakers and play your chosen music.

Lessening the lighting in the room can help in releasing your inhibitions; leaving you freer to dance like there is no tomorrow, forgetting any stress that you have to deal with in your life. The blaring music will also help in blocking out any distracting thoughts trying to bring you back to a state of distress. Enjoy this little time you have and shake those arms! Wiggle those hips! Stomp your feet (but do be wary of neighbors)!

Chapter 7 - The Help of Health

Stress is a common factor in the expression of diseases like cancer. It is also a surefire way of downing your body's defenses against bad elements found around us. In order to combat stress and its ill effects, take the proactive step and take care of your health.

You are probably thinking that you are in too deep in your unhealthy ways, but for as long as you are alive, you still have a chance to turn your life around and do what is best for your body.

67

Some common ways of combating stress by becoming more health-conscious are:

1.) Exercise daily

Not only does physical activity combat the effects of stress, it is also a way of releasing any inner tension you are experiencing. While exercising, you are most likely to be distracted by the need to breathe so you will be able to temporarily forget whatever has been bothering you. And endorphins, your body's feel-good neurotransmitters, are produced during exercise.

Exercising can seem like a chore at first, so do not go all in right away. Try gradually adding to your routine as time passes. You may opt to do some gentler workouts like Pilates or Yoga. Working out with a friend can also be a motivating factor.

Using the method of changing your environment, dress yourself up for your workout when going to bed. What is important is that you work towards a goal that is attainable while employing methods that will create an optimal environment and atmosphere for regular exercise.

2.) Eat a balanced diet

Stressed out people have probably been skipping out on breakfast for most of their grown-up lives. Some others may be eating food so colorful save for the green of nutritious vegetables. This is what a modernized, fast-food-crazed society has done to us.

Eating healthy and balanced meals throughout your day makes all the difference in equipping you with the needed nutrients to fight the bad effects of stress. Do not skip on breakfast and keep your healthy streak throughout the day with some room for a treat on the side, of course.

3.) Lessen your sugar and caffeine intake

Reading the title of this very section may have caused you stress but lowering the amount of sugar and caffeine from the snacks and beverages you take in throughout the day can help avoid the eventual mood and energy crash caused by the momentary "highs" these substances bring.

Not only will you be more relaxed, but you will be able to sleep better as well, avoiding any bouts of insomnia or extra nervousness. This is easier said than done, though, especially for people who consider themselves to have a sweet tooth.

If you find yourselves craving for some savory sweet treat, try eating fruits instead. For instance, you may sweeten iced tea by using fruit juice instead of resorting to a ready mix filled with sugar. Now you are not just making yourself feel relaxed but are also doing something beneficial for your health.

4.) No to alcohol, drugs, and cigarettes

It is true that using these substances can bring some stress relief but this is only temporary at best. All the toxins are not worth it. For as much as you can, deal with your problems with a clear mind instead of being all jacked up on these substances.

Becoming dependent on these substances also creates an added stress for you and those around you. Your resistance to diseases will be lowered, harming your health. The solid link between lung cancer and smoking should be enough of a warning to you.

In the event that alcohol intake cannot be resisted, just remember to have a trusted and very sober friend with you who can take care of you when you get drunk.

5.) Need for sleep

Getting enough sleep can help energize you for when you need to take on the challenges that life may bring during the day. A tired mind borne out of a lack of sleep can make you irrational and, thus, unable to adequately deal with stress.

Try these:

1.) Put Garlic on Everything

Garlic has been proven to relax blood vessels and enhance the flow of blood in our bodies, making hearts healthier and more able to manage stress. Garlic is cheap and can be put on almost any dish. Think of pasta, sauces, soup, and garlic bread! The possibilities are endless and so will be your capacity to handle stress thanks to the wonders of garlic!

2.) Sleep with your phone away from you

This method of coping has been the talk of the town for some time, or at least since cellular phones became a must-have for everyone. Some even refer to this very method as a life hack.

What you should do is to put your phone at a considerable distance from your bed. This helps in waking you up more than having your phone beside you because you need to get up and walk a bit to turn your phone's alarm off. You are significantly more awakened and you are less likely to fall back asleep when you use this method.

Another pro to putting your phone away from you and your bed is that it lessens exposure to the harmful radiation waves your phone emits. While it is still being disputed just how impactful these waves are to your health, some experts liken sleeping right next to your phone to frying your brain. So to stay on the safe side, it would be best to start getting used to sleeping without your phone beside you.

3.) Straighten up

Practicing good posture is another way of relieving stress. Do this by staying away from doing the slumping position. Why? Slumping, an indicator of stress, has been found to restrict breathing. It also affects the flow of blood and oxygen to the brain which results to intensified tension in the muscles and feelings of helplessness.

By straightening your spine, you are promoting the blood and oxygen flow in your body, contributing to an overall sense of calm and relaxation.

4.) Load on Carbs

Carbohydrate-rich foods help stimulate the release of serotonin, a neurotransmitter that induces a feeling of calm in an individual. Have some bread or biscuits on the ready especially for situations where you anticipate heightened stress levels.

5.) Stretch!

The tightening of muscles throughout the day is enhanced further by stress, so stretch those muscles and take breaths so deep you will forget the stress you were just experiencing.

CONCLUSION

Thank you again for downloading this book!

You have now reached the end of this book. Throughout your reading, you have been given the basics and some ideas on how to come up with your own strategies for coping with the numerous stressors you encounter every day.

Which strategy did you find most suitable to how you are as a person? Was it the use of avoidance in dealing with manageable stressors? Or was it the use of acceptance when it comes to stressors borne out of unchangeable circumstances? Maybe you found the external change section the easiest or most effective for you. Or perhaps it was the steps listed under internal change?

No matter which strategy you have chosen, you should be commended for taking initiative to rid yourself of all the stress in your life by choosing this book as a reference in your continuing journey of finding which coping strategies will work best for you.

If you happen to feel a case of information overload, that is understandable. This book was quite packed with coping strategies, anyway. Do not fret, though. You can always take a gander at the book for times when you feel confused or when you want to change something about your chosen coping strategy.

The most important thing to remember as you peruse this book and its contents for a better life is to be patient with yourself. There will be times when you will go back to your old ways of ineffective and temporary coping. Do not think of your relapses to old habits as a failure.

Instead, as iterated in an earlier chapter, every step you take in your quest to becoming a more balanced person, whether it be a step forward or backward, is a step nonetheless. All you need is some support from those around you to get you going.

And should you find yourself alone in this journey, do not be upset too much. A lot of people feel the exact same way. What differs you from the rest, though, is how exactly you will cope with the unique stressors that come your way. This book will be with you every step of the way. So, which step will you be taking, a step forward or back? You decide.

Finally, if you enjoyed this book, then I'd like to ask you for a favor, would you be kind enough to leave a review for this book on Amazon? It'd be greatly appreciated!

Click here to leave a review for this book on Amazon! Thank you and good luck!